Knit
prayer shawls
15 Wraps to Share

Prayer shawls are the most heartfelt of gifts. They convey the knitter's best wishes for the happiness and health of friends and family, as well as strangers in need. Eleven of the knitting industry's most popular designers created these exclusive patterns. This handy book slips easily into a purse or workbag, so you can work on a prayer shawl wherever you go. With your love and prayers knitted into every stitch, your gift will become a cherished keepsake.

LEISURE ARTS, INC.
Maumelle, Arkansas

Library of Congress Control Number: 2010923373

ISBN-13: 978-1-60900-001-1

table of contents

Southwest color

Finished Size: 19"w x 70"l
(48.5 cm x 178 cm) blocked

Cynthia Guggemos
Cynthia created this lovely gift of compassion with a spicy red yarn that's sure to inspire happiness each time it's worn. The motif of cascading leaves is enhanced by the lacy border.

MATERIALS

Medium Weight Yarn
[3 ounces, 158 yards
(85 grams, 144 meters)
per skein]: 5 skeins
24" (61 cm) Circular knitting
needle, size 9 (5.5 mm) **or**
size needed for gauge
Markers

*Photo model made
using Lion Brand®
Lion® Wool #102
Ranch Red.*

*Instructions continued
on page 6.*

GAUGE: In Stockinette Stitch,
14 sts and 20 rows = 4" (10 cm) before blocking

Techniques used: • Slip 1 as if to **knit**, K2 tog, PSSO
(Figs. 6a & b, page 91); • K2 tog *(Fig. 4, page 90)*;
• SSK *(Figs. 10a-c, page 93)*; • M1 *(Figs. 2a & b, page 88)*;
and • YO *(Fig. 3a, page 88)*

FIRST BORDER

Cast on 61 sts.

Rows 1-6: Knit across.

Row 7: K8, M1, K 45, M1, K8: 63 sts.

Row 8 (Right side): K9, place marker *(see Markers, page 87)*
(side border), K 45, place marker (side border), K9.

Row 9: K9, slip marker, P 45, slip marker, K9.

Row 10: K9, slip marker, K3, † YO, SSK, K3,YO, slip 1 as if to **knit**, K2 tog, PSSO,YO, K3, K2 tog,YO †, K5,YO, slip 1 as if to **knit**, K2 tog, PSSO,YO, K5, repeat from † to † once, K3, slip marker, K9.

Row 11: K9, slip marker, P 45, slip marker, K9.

Row 12: K9, slip marker, K3, † YO, SSK, K2,YO, SSK, K1, K2 tog, YO, K2, K2 tog,YO †, K4,YO, SSK, K1, K2 tog,YO, K4, repeat from † to † once, K3, slip marker, K9.

Row 13: K9, slip marker, P 45, slip marker, K9.

Rows 14-35: Repeat Rows 10-13, 5 times; then repeat Rows 10 and 11 once **more**.

Rows 36-43: Knit across.

BODY

Row 1: K3,YO, SSK, K1, K2 tog,YO, K1, slip marker, K6, | K2 tog,YO, K3,YO, SSK †, K2,YO, K2, SSK, P7, K2 tog, K2,YO, K2, repeat from † to † once, K6, slip marker, K1,YO, SSK, K1, K2 tog,YO, K3.

Row 2 AND ALL WRONG SIDE ROWS: K9, slip marker, P 45, slip marker, K9.

Row 3: K4,YO, slip 1 as if to **knit**, K2 tog, PSSO,YO, K2, slip marker, K5, † K2 tog,YO, K1,YO, slip 1 as if to **knit**, K2 tog, PSSO,YO, K1,YO, SSK †, K2,YO, K2, SSK, P5, K2 tog, K2,YO, K2, repeat from † to † once, K5, slip marker, K2,YO, slip 1 as if to **knit**, K2 tog, PSSO,YO, K4.

Instructions continued on page 8.

Row 5: K3, YO, SSK, K1, K2 tog, YO, K1, slip marker, K4, † K2 tog, YO, K1, YO, SSK, K1, K2 tog, YO, K1, YO, SSK †, K2, YO, K2, SSK, P3, K2 tog, K2, YO, K2, repeat from † to † once, K4, slip marker, K1, YO, SSK, K1, K2 tog, YO, K3.

Row 7: K4, YO, slip 1 as if to **knit**, K2 tog, PSSO, YO, K2, slip marker, K3, † K2 tog, YO, K3, YO, slip 1 as if to **knit**, K2 tog, PSSO, YO, K3, YO, SSK †, K2, YO, K2, SSK, P1, K2 tog, K2, YO, K2, repeat from † to † once, K3, slip marker, K2, YO, slip 1 as if to **knit**, K2 tog, PSSO, YO, K4.

Row 9: K3, YO, SSK, K1, K2 tog, YO, K1, slip marker, K5, P9, K5, YO, K2, slip 1 as if to **knit**, K2 tog, PSSO, K2, YO, K5, P9, K5, slip marker, K1, YO, SSK, K1, K2 tog, YO, K3.

Row 11: K4, YO, slip 1 as if to **knit**, K2 tog, PSSO, YO, K2, slip marker, K2, † YO, K2, SSK, P7, K2 tog, K2, YO †, K2, K2 tog, YO, K3, YO, SSK, K2, repeat from † to † once, K2, slip marker, K2, YO, slip 1 as if to **knit**, K2 tog, PSSO, YO, K4.

Row 13: K3, YO, SSK, K1, K2 tog, YO, K1, slip marker, K3, † YO, K2, SSK, P5, K2 tog, K2, YO †, K2, K2 tog, YO, K1, YO, slip 1 as if to **knit**, K2 tog, PSSO, YO, K1, YO, SSK, K2, repeat from † to † once, K3, slip marker, K1, YO, SSK, K1, K2 tog, YO, K3.

Row 15: K4, YO, slip 1 as if to **knit**, K2 tog, PSSO, YO, K2, slip marker, K4, † YO, K2, SSK, P3, K2 tog, K2, YO †, K2, K2 tog, YO, K1, YO, SSK, K1, K2 tog, YO, K1, YO, SSK, K2, repeat from † to † once, K4, slip marker, K2, YO, slip 1 as if to **knit**, K2 tog, PSSO, YO, K4.

Row 17: K3, YO, SSK, K1, K2 tog, YO, K1, slip marker, K5, † YO, K2, SSK, P1, K2 tog, K2, YO †, K2, K2 tog, YO, K3, YO, slip 1 as if to **knit**, K2 tog, PSSO, YO, K3, YO, SSK, K2, repeat from † to † once, K5, slip marker, K1, YO, SSK, K1, K2 tog, YO, K3.

Row 19: K4, YO, slip 1 as if to **knit**, K2 tog, PSSO, YO, K2, slip marker, K6, † YO, K2, slip 1 as if to **knit**, K2 tog, PSSO, K2, YO †, K5, P9, K5, repeat from † to † once, K6, slip marker, K2, YO, slip 1 as if to **knit**, K2 tog, PSSO, YO, K4.

Rows 21-259: Repeat Rows 1-20, 11 times; then repeat Rows 1-19 once **more**.

SECOND BORDER

Rows 1-8: Knit across.

Rows 9-35: Work same as First Border.

Row 36: Knit across.

Row 37: K7, SSK, remove marker, K 45, remove marker, K2 tog, K7: 61 sts.

Rows 38-43: Knit across.

Bind off all sts in **knit**.

Just-Right wrap

Lisa Ellis

The softly waving pattern of Lisa's long wrap is airy and open, a perfect comfort for days when the warmth of your friendship can make all the difference.

Finished Size: 14"w x 71¹/₂"l (35.5 cm x 181.5 cm)

MATERIALS

MEDIUM
4

Medium Weight Yarn [3.5 ounces, 220 yards (100 grams, 201 meters) per ball]: 4 balls

36" (91.5 cm) Circular knitting needle, size 7 (4.5 mm) **or** size needed for gauge

Photo model made using Cascade Yarns® 220 Superwash #803.

Instructions continued on page 12.

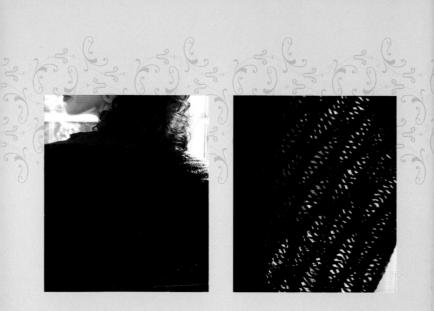

GAUGE: In Stockinette Stitch, 20 sts = 4" (10 cm)

In pattern, 17 sts = 4" (10 cm)

Techniques used: • YO *(Fig. 3a, page 88)* and • YO twice *(Fig. A, page 80)*

BODY

Cast on 304 sts.

Rows 1-4: Knit across.

Row 5: K4, ★ (YO, K1) 3 times, (YO twice, K1) 3 times, YO, (K1, YO) twice, K4; repeat from ★ across: 604 sts.

Row 6: K4, ★ (drop YO, K1) 3 times, (drop 2 YO, K1) 3 times, drop YO, (K1, drop YO) twice, K4; repeat from ★ across: 304 sts.

Rows 7-10: Knit across.

Row 11: K4, (YO, K1) twice, YO, ★ K4, (YO, K1) 3 times, (YO twice, K1) 3 times, YO, (K1, YO) twice; repeat from ★ across to last 10 sts, K4, YO, (K1, YO) twice, K4: 598 sts.

Row 12: K4, (drop YO, K1) twice, drop YO, ★ K4, (drop YO, K1) 3 times, (drop 2 YO, K1) 3 times, drop YO, (K1, drop YO) twice; repeat from ★ across to last 13 sts, K4, drop YO, (K1, drop YO) twice, K4: 304 sts.

Rows 13-99: Repeat Rows 1-12, 7 times; then repeat Rows 1-3 once **more**.

Bind off all sts **loosely** in **knit**.

 **INTERMEDIATE**

Finished Size: 51"w x 25" deep
(129.5 cm x 63.5 cm)

MATERIALS

Light Weight Yarn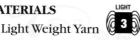
[2.5 ounces, 168 yards
(70 grams, 154 meters)
per skein]: 5 skeins
29" (73.5 cm) Circular knitting
needle, size 9 (5.5 mm) **or**
size needed for gauge

Lisa Gentry
A kind gift of
caring, Lisa's
half-circle shawl
seems to flare
from the shoulders
before ending in
gentle scallops.
In this sweet
vanilla color, it is
reminiscent of the
softest rays
of sunshine.

*Photo model made
using Lion Brand®
Microspun #098
French Vanilla.*

*Instructions continued
on page 16.*

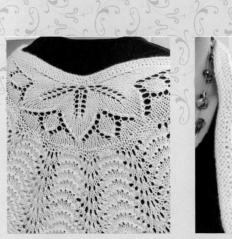

GAUGE: In Stockinette Stitch,
20 sts and 28 rows = 4" (10 cm)

Techniques used: • Increase *(Figs. 1a & b, page 87)*;
• YO *(Figs. 3a, c, & d, pages 88 and 89)*; • Slip 1 as if to
knit, K1, PSSO *(Fig. 7, page 91)*; • Slip 1 as if to **knit**, K2 tog,
PSSO *(Figs. 6a & b, page 91)*; • K2 tog *(Fig. 4, page 90)*; and
• P2 tog *(Fig. 5, page 90)*

BODY

Cast on 6 sts.

Row 1 AND ALL WRONG SIDE ROWS through Row 27:
Purl across.

Row 2 (Right side): (K1, YO) 5 times, K1: 11 sts.

Row 4: K2, YO, (K1, YO) 7 times, K2: 19 sts.

Row 6: K2, YO, K3, YO, (K1, YO, K3, YO) 3 times, K2: 27 sts.

Row 8: K2, YO, K5, YO, (K1, YO, K5, YO) 3 times, K2: 35 sts.

Row 10: K2, YO, K7, YO, (K1, YO, K7, YO) 3 times, K2: 43 sts.

Row 12: K2, YO, K9, YO, (K1, YO, K9, YO) 3 times, K2: 51 sts.

Row 14: K2, YO, K 11, YO, (K1, YO, K 11, YO) 3 times, K2: 59 sts.

Row 16: K6, ★ † K2 tog, YO, K1, YO, slip 1 as if to **knit**, K1, PSSO †, K9; repeat from ★ 2 times **more**, then repeat from † to † once, K6.

Row 18: K5, ★ † K2 tog, YO, K3, YO, slip 1 as if to **knit**, K1, PSSO †, K7; repeat from ★ 2 times **more**, then repeat from † to † once, K5.

Row 20: K4, ★ † K2 tog, YO, K5, YO, slip 1 as if to **knit**, K1, PSSO †, K5; repeat from ★ 2 times **more**, then repeat from † to † once, K4.

Row 22: K3, ★ K2 tog, YO, K1, YO, K5, YO, K1, YO, slip 1 as if to **knit**, K1, PSSO, K3; repeat from ★ across: 67 sts.

Row 24: K2, ★ † K2 tog, YO, K3, YO, slip 1 as if to **knit**, K1, PSSO, K1, K2 tog, YO, K3, YO, slip 1 as if to **knit**, K1, PSSO †, K1; repeat from ★ 2 times **more**, then repeat from † to † once, K2.

Row 26: ★ K1, K2 tog, YO, K5, YO, slip 1 as if to **knit**, K2 tog, PSSO, YO, K5, YO; repeat from ★ across to last 3 sts, K3: 71 sts.

Instructions continued on page 18.

Row 28: K 17, K2 tog, (K 15, K2 tog) 3 times, K1: 67 sts.

Row 29: Purl across.

Row 30: Knit across increasing 11 sts evenly spaced across: 78 sts.

Row 31: Knit across.

Row 32: Knit across increasing 14 sts evenly spaced across: 92 sts.

Rows 33-35: Knit across.

Row 36: K2, P3, YO, (K1, YO) 5 times, ★ P6, YO, (K1, YO) 5 times; repeat from ★ across to last 5 sts, P3, K2: 140 sts.

Row 37: Purl across.

Row 38: Knit across.

Row 39: Purl across.

Row 40: K2, P2 tog 3 times, YO, (K1, YO) 5 times, ★ P2 tog 6 times, YO, (K1, YO) 5 times; repeat from ★ across to last 8 sts, P2 tog 3 times, K2.

Rows 41-43: Repeat Rows 37-39.

Row 44: K2, P1, P2 tog twice, (K1, YO) 6 times, K1, ★ P1, P2 tog 4 times, P1, (K1, YO) 6 times, K1; repeat from ★ across to last 7 sts, P2 tog twice, P1, K2: 156 sts.

Rows 45-47: Repeat Rows 37-39.

Row 48: K2, P2 tog 3 times, (K1, YO) 6 times, K1, ★ P2 tog 6 times, (K1, YO) 6 times, K1; repeat from ★ across to last 8 sts, P2 tog 3 times, K2.

Rows 49-51: Repeat Rows 37-39.

Row 52: K2, P2 tog 3 times, (K1, YO) 6 times, K1, ★ P2 tog 6 times, (K1, YO) 6 times, K1; repeat from ★ across to last 8 sts, P2 tog 3 times, K2.

Rows 53-55: Repeat Rows 37-39.

Row 56: K2, P2 tog 3 times, YO, (K1, YO) 7 times, ★ P2 tog 6 times, YO, (K1, YO) 7 times; repeat from ★ across to last 8 sts, P2 tog 3 times, K2: 172 sts.

Rows 57-59: Repeat Rows 37-39.

Row 60: K2, P2 tog 3 times, K1, (YO, K1) 8 times, ★ P2 tog 6 times, K1, (YO, K1) 8 times; repeat from ★ across to last 8 sts, P2 tog 3 times, K2: 188 sts.

Rows 61-63: Repeat Rows 37-39.

Row 64: K2, P2 tog 4 times, YO, (K1, YO) 7 times, ★ P2 tog 8 times, YO, (K1, YO) 7 times; repeat from ★ across to last 10 sts, P2 tog 4 times, K2.

Rows 65-67: Repeat Rows 37-39.

Row 68: K2, P1, P2 tog 3 times, K1, (YO, K1) 8 times, ★ P1, P2 tog 6 times, P1, K1, (YO, K1) 8 times; repeat from ★ across to last 9 sts, P2 tog 3 times, P1, K2: 204 sts.

Instructions continued on page 20.

Rows 69-71: Repeat Rows 37-39.

Row 72: K2, P2 tog 4 times, (K1, YO) 8 times, K1, ★ P2 tog 8 times, (K1, YO) 8 times, K1; repeat from ★ across to last 10 sts, P2 tog 4 times, K2.

Rows 73-75: Repeat Rows 37-39.

Row 76: K2, P2 tog 4 times, YO, (K1, YO) 9 times, ★ P2 tog 8 times, YO, (K1, YO) 9 times; repeat from ★ across to last 10 sts, P2 tog 4 times, K2: 220 sts.

Rows 77-79: Repeat Rows 37-39.

Row 80: K2, P2 tog 4 times, YO, (K1, YO) 11 times, ★ P2 tog 8 times, YO, (K1, YO) 11 times; repeat from ★ across to last 10 sts, P2 tog 4 times, K2: 252 sts.

Rows 81-83: Repeat Rows 37-39.

Row 84: K2, P2 tog 5 times, YO, (K1, YO) 11 times, ★ P2 tog 10 times, YO, (K1, YO) 11 times; repeat from ★ across to last 12 sts, P2 tog 5 times, K2: 268 sts.

Rows 85-87: Repeat Rows 37-39.

Row 88: K2, P2 tog 5 times, K1, (YO, K1) 12 times, ★ P2 tog 10 times, K1, (YO, K1) 12 times; repeat from ★ across to last 12 sts, P2 tog 5 times, K2: 284 sts.

Rows 89-91: Repeat Rows 37-39.

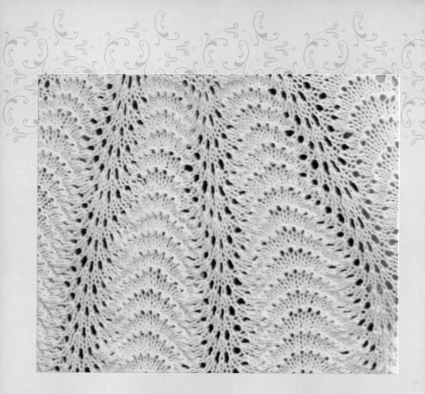

Row 92: K2, P2 tog 6 times, YO, (K1, YO) 11 times, ★ P2 tog 12 times, YO, (K1, YO) 11 times; repeat from ★ across to last 14 sts, P2 tog 6 times, K2: 284 sts.

Rows 93-95: Repeat Rows 37-39.

Row 96: K2, P1, P2 tog 5 times, YO, (K1, YO) 13 times, ★ P1, P2 tog 10 times, P1, YO, (K1, YO) 13 times; repeat from ★ across to last 13 sts, P2 tog 5 times, P1, K2: 316 sts.

Rows 97-99: Repeat Rows 37-39.

Row 100: K2, P1, P2 tog 6 times, YO, (K1, YO) 13 times, ★ P1, P2 tog 12 times, P1, YO, (K1, YO) 13 times; repeat from ★ across to last 15 sts, P2 tog 6 times, P1, K2: 332 sts.

Rows 101-103: Repeat Rows 37-39.

Instructions continued on page 22.

Row 104: K2, P2 tog 7 times, YO, (K1, YO) 13 times, ★ P2 tog 14 times, YO, (K1, YO) 13 times; repeat from ★ across to last 16 sts, P2 tog 7 times, K2.

Rows 105-107: Repeat Rows 37-39.

Row 108: Repeat Row 104.

Rows 109-111: Repeat Rows 37-39.

Row 112: K2, P2 tog 6 times, K1, (YO, K1) 16 times, ★ P2 tog 12 times, K1, (YO, K1) 16 times; repeat from ★ across to last 14 sts, P2 tog 6 times, K2: 364 sts.

Rows 113-115: Repeat Rows 37-39.

Row 116: K2, P2 tog 7 times, YO, (K1, YO) 17 times, ★ P2 tog 14 times, YO, (K1, YO) 17 times; repeat from ★ across to last 16 sts, P2 tog 7 times, K2: 396 sts.

Rows 117-121: Knit across.

Bind off all sts **loosely** in **knit**, leaving last st on needle; do **not** cut yarn.

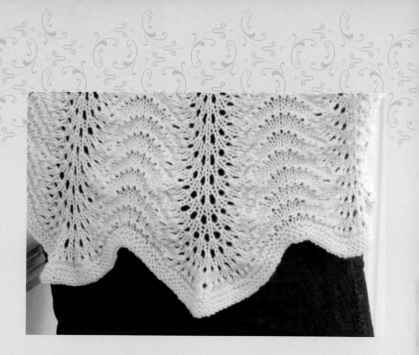

EDGING

With **right** side facing, pick up 126 sts evenly spaced across end of rows to cast on, pick up 6 sts across cast on *(Figs. A & B)*, pick up 126 sts across opposite end of rows: 258 sts.

Rows 1-5: Knit across.

Bind off all sts **loosely** in **knit**.

Fig. A

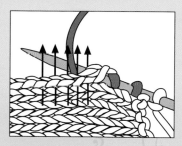

Fig. B

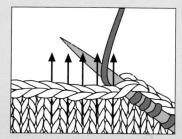

Comfort abides

■■■□ **INTERMEDIATE**

Finished Size: 63"w x 30"l
(160 cm x 76 cm)

MATERIALS
Medium Weight Yarn
  [3.5 ounces, 218 yards,
  (100 grams 200 meters)
  per skein]: 2 skeins
24" (61 cm) Circular knitting
  needle, size 10¹/₂ (6.5 mm) **or**
  size needed for gauge

Lisa Gentry
A variegated
yarn in earthy
hues makes this
triangular shawl a
comforting sight
that will always
remind her of your
thoughtfulness.

*Photo model made
using Red Heart®
Collage™ #2940 Wood
Trail.*

*Instructions continued
on page 26.*

GAUGE: In pattern,
    15 sts = 5" (12.75 cm);
    20 rows = 4" (10 cm)

Techniques used: • Increase *(Figs. 1a & b, page 87)*; • YO *(Fig. 3a, page 88)*; • Slip 1 as if to **knit**, K1, PSSO *(Fig. 7, page 91)*; • Slip 1 as if to **knit**, K2 tog, PSSO *(Figs. 6a & b, page 91)*; and • K2 tog *(Fig. 4, page 90)*

BODY

Cast on 3 sts.

Row 1: Knit across.

Rows 2-4: Increase, knit across to last st, increase: 9 sts.

Row 5: Knit across.

Row 6 (Right side): K2,YO,K2 tog,YO,K1,YO,slip 1 as if to **knit**,K1,PSSO,YO,K2: 11 sts.

Row 7 AND ALL WRONG SIDE ROWS: K2, purl across to last 2 sts, K2.

Row 8: K2,YO,K2 tog,YO,K3,YO, slip 1 as if to **knit**,K1,PSSO, YO,K2: 13 sts.

Row 10: K2,YO,(K2 tog,YO) twice,K1,(YO,slip 1 as if to **knit**,K1,PSSO) twice,YO,K2: 15 sts.

Row 12: K2,YO,(K2 tog,YO) twice,K3,(YO,slip 1 as if to **knit**,K1,PSSO) twice,YO,K2: 17 sts.

Row 14: K2,(YO,K1) twice,YO,slip 1 as if to **knit**,K1,PSSO, K5,K2 tog,(YO,K1) twice,YO,K2: 21 sts.

Row 16: K2,YO,K2 tog,YO,K3,YO, slip 1 as if to **knit**,K1, PSSO,K3,K2 tog,YO,K3,YO,slip 1 as if to **knit**,K1,PSSO,YO, K2: 23 sts.

Row 18: K2,YO,(K2 tog,YO) twice,K1,(YO,slip 1 as if to **knit**,K1,PSSO) twice,K1,(K2 tog,YO) twice,K1,(YO,slip 1 as if to **knit**,K1,PSSO) twice,YO,K2: 25 sts.

Row 20: K2,YO,(K2 tog,YO) twice,K3,YO,slip 1 as if to **knit**, K1,PSSO,YO,slip 1 as if to **knit**,K2 tog,PSSO,YO,K2 tog,YO, K3,(YO,slip 1 as if to **knit**,K1,PSSO) twice,YO,K2: 27 sts.

Instructions continued on page 28.

Row 22: K2, (YO, K1) twice, ★ YO, slip 1 as if to **knit**, K1, PSSO, K5, K2 tog, YO, K1; repeat from ★ once **more**; YO, K1, YO, K2: 31 sts.

Row 24: K2, YO, ★ † K2 tog, YO, K3, YO, slip 1 as if to **knit**, K1, PSSO †, K3; repeat from ★ once **more**, then repeat from † to † once, YO, K2: 33 sts.

Row 26: K2, YO, ★ † (K2 tog, YO) twice, K1, (YO, slip 1 as if to **knit**, K1, PSSO) twice †, K1; repeat from ★ once **more**, then repeat from † to † once, YO, K2: 35 sts.

Row 28: K2, YO, (K2 tog, YO) twice, K3, ★ YO, slip 1 as if to **knit**, K1, PSSO, YO, slip 1 as if to **knit**, K2 tog, PSSO, YO, K2 tog, YO, K3; repeat from ★ once **more**, (YO, slip 1 as if to **knit**, K1, PSSO) twice, YO, K2: 37 sts.

Row 30: K2, (YO, K1) twice, ★ YO, slip 1 as if to **knit**, K1, PSSO, K5, K2 tog, YO, K1; repeat from ★ across to last 3 sts, YO, K1, YO, K2: 41 sts.

Row 32: K2, YO, ★ † K2 tog, YO, K3, YO, slip 1 as if to **knit**, K1, PSSO †, K3; repeat from ★ across to last 9 sts, then repeat from † to † once, YO, K2: 43 sts.

Row 34: K2, YO, ★ † (K2 tog, YO) twice, K1, (YO, slip 1 as if to **knit**, K1, PSSO) twice †, K1; repeat from ★ across to last 11 sts, then repeat from † to † once, YO, K2: 45 sts.

Row 36: K2, YO, (K2 tog, YO) twice, K3, ★ YO, slip 1 as if to **knit**, K1, PSSO, YO, slip 1 as if to **knit**, K2 tog, PSSO, YO, K2 tog, YO, K3; repeat from ★ across to last 6 sts, (YO, slip 1 as if to **knit**, K1, PSSO) twice, YO, K2: 47 sts.

Rows 38-149: Repeat Rows 30-37, 14 times: 187 sts.

Rows 150-154: Knit across.

Bind off **loosely** in **knit**.

◼◼◼◻ **INTERMEDIATE**

Finished Size: 72"w x 20"l (183 cm x 51 cm) excluding fringe

MATERIALS

Medium Weight Yarn
[1.41 ounces, 100 yards (40 grams, 92 meters) per hank]: 5 hanks
29" (73.5 cm) Circular knitting needle, size 8 (5 mm) **or** size needed for gauge
Marker
Crochet hook for fringe

Jeannine LaRoche
This darling V-shaped shawl is worked from the top edges down to the bottom. Although it is knitted using medium weight yarn, Jeannine's openwork pattern creates a wrap that's light as a whisper and warmed with prayers.

Photo model made using Berroco® Seduce® #4448 Verdigris.

Instructions continued on page 32.

GAUGE: In pattern, 20 sts and 34 rows = 4" (10 cm)

Techniques used: • Increase *(Figs. 1a & b, page 87)*;
• YO *(Fig. 3a, page 88)*; and • K2 tog *(Fig. 4, page 90)*

BODY

Cast on 105 sts, place marker *(see Markers, page 87)*, cast on another 105 sts: 210 sts.

Row 1 AND ALL ODD-NUMBERED ROWS: Knit across.

Rows 2, 4, 6 and 8: K2 tog, knit across to within one st of marker, increase, slip marker, increase, knit across to last 2 sts, K2 tog.

Row 10: (K2 tog, YO) across to within one st of marker, K1, slip marker, K1, (YO, K2 tog) across.

Rows 11-99: Repeat Rows 1-10, 8 times; then repeat Rows 1-9 once **more**.

Row 100: (K2 tog, YO) across to within one st of marker, K1, remove marker, YO, K1, (YO, K2 tog) across.

Rows 101 and 102: Knit across.

Bind off all sts in **knit**.

FRINGE

Holding 3 strands of yarn together, each 10" (25.5 cm) long, add fringe to each YO along lower edge of Shawl *(Figs. 11a & b, page 94)*.

Colors of joy

Finished Size: 60"w x 32"l
(152.5 cm x 81.5 cm) excluding
fringe

MATERIALS

Fine Weight Yarn
[3.5 ounces, 330 yards
(100 grams, 302 meters)
per skein]: 2 skeins
24" (61 cm) Circular knitting
needle, size 8 (5 mm) **or**
size needed for gauge
Crochet hook for fringe

*Jeannine
LaRoche*
Color to cheer
her—this happy
shawl uses a
vibrant, variegated
yarn to convey
your best wishes
for a joyous future.

*Photo model made
using Noro Silk Garden
Sock Yarn #279
Browns/Blues/Deep
Rose.*

*Instructions continued
on page 36.*

GAUGE: In pattern, 16 sts and 28 rows = 4" (10 cm)

Techniques used: • YO *(Fig. 3a, page 88)* and • Slip 1 as if to **knit**, K2 tog, PSSO *(Figs. 6a & b, page 91)*

BODY
Cast on 4 sts.

Rows 1 and 2: Knit across.

Row 3 (Right side): K2, YO, K2: 5 sts.

Row 4: K2, P1, K2.

Row 5: K2, YO, K1, YO, K2: 7 sts.

Row 6: K2, P3, K2.

Row 7: K2, YO, K3, YO, K2: 9 sts.

Row 8 AND ALL WRONG SIDE ROWS: K2, purl across to last 2 sts, K2.

Row 9: K2, YO, K5, YO, K2: 11 sts.

Row 11: K2, YO, K7, YO, K2: 13 sts.

Row 13: K2, YO, K9, YO, K2: 15 sts.

Row 15: K2, YO, K1, YO, K3, slip 1 as if to **knit**, K2 tog, PSSO, K3, YO, K1, YO, K2: 17 sts.

Row 17: K2, YO, K3, YO, K2, slip 1 as if to **knit**, K2 tog, PSSO, K2, YO, K3, YO, K2: 19 sts.

Row 19: K2, YO, K5, YO, K1, slip 1 as if to **knit**, K2 tog, PSSO, K1, YO, K5, YO, K2: 21 sts.

Row 21: K2, YO, K7, YO, slip 1 as if to **knit**, K2 tog, PSSO, YO, K7, YO, K2: 23 sts.

Row 23: K2, YO, K1, † YO, K2, slip 1 as if to **knit**, K2 tog, PSSO, K2, YO †, K3, repeat from † to † once, K1, YO, K2: 25 sts.

Row 25: K2, YO, K3, † YO, K1, slip 1 as if to **knit**, K2 tog, PSSO, K1, YO †, K5, repeat from † to † once, K3, YO, K2: 27 sts.

Row 27: K2, YO, K5, † YO, slip 1 as if to **knit**, K2 tog, PSSO, YO †, K7, repeat from † to † once, K5, YO, K2: 29 sts.

Row 29: K2, YO, K7, YO, K1, YO, K3, slip 1 as if to **knit**, K2 tog, PSSO, K3, YO, K1, YO, K7, YO, K2: 33 sts.

Instructions continued on page 82.

Celtic Spirit

◼◼◼◻ INTERMEDIATE

Jill Wright
Anyone wearing
Jill's swathe of
comforting blue
cables is sure to
feel lighthearted.
She'll also feel
blessed by true
friendship.

Finished Size: 12"w x 56"l
(30.5 cm x 142 cm) excluding
fringe

MATERIALS

Medium Weight Yarn
[3.5 ounces, 215 yards
(100 grams, 198 meters)
per hank]: 5 hanks
Straight knitting needles, size 8
(5 mm) **or** size needed
for gauge
Cable needle
Crochet hook for fringe

*Photo model made
using Berroco® Ultra®
Alpaca #6239 Pastel
Blue.*

*Instructions continued
on page 40.*

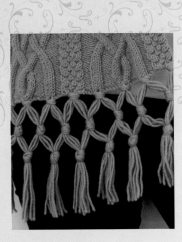

GAUGE: In Stockinette Stitch,
22 sts and 28 rows = 4" (10 cm)

STITCH GUIDE

CABLE 4 FRONT *(abbreviated C4F)* (uses 4 sts)
Slip next 2 sts onto cable needle and hold in **front** of
work, K2 from left needle, K2 from cable needle.

CABLE 4 BACK *(abbreviated C4B)* (uses 4 sts)
Slip next 2 sts onto cable needle and hold in **back** of
work, K2 from left needle, K2 from cable needle.

CABLE 6 FRONT *(abbreviated C6F)* (uses 6 sts)
Slip next 3 sts onto cable needle and hold in **front** of
work, K3 from left needle, K3 from cable needle.

CABLE 6 BACK *(abbreviated C6B)* (uses 6 sts)
Slip next 3 sts onto cable needle and hold in **back** of
work, K3 from left needle, K3 from cable needle.

TWIST 4 LEFT *(abbreviated T4L)* (uses 4 sts)
Slip next 3 sts onto cable needle and hold in **front** of
work, P1 from left needle, K3 from cable needle.

TWIST 4 RIGHT *(abbreviated T4R)* (uses 4 sts)
Slip next st onto cable needle and hold in **back** of work,
K3 sts from left needle, P1 from cable needle.

BODY

Cast on 92 sts.

Row 1 (Right side)**:** Slip 1 as if to **purl**, K2, C4F twice, ★ P3, K3, P6, C6B, P6, K3, P3, K2, C4F twice; repeat from ★ once **more**, P1.

Row 2: Slip 1 as if to **knit**, P 10, ★ K3, P3, K6, P6, K6, P3, K3, P 10; repeat from ★ once **more**, K1.

Row 3: Slip 1 as if to **purl**, C4B twice, K2, ★ P3, K3, P5, T4R, T4L, P5, K3, P3, C4B twice, K2; repeat from ★ once **more**, P1.

Row 4: Slip 1 as if to **knit**, P 10, ★ K3, P3, K5, P3, K2, P3, K5, P3, K3, P 10; repeat from ★ once **more**, K1.

Row 5: Slip 1 as if to **purl**, K2, C4F twice, ★ P3, K3, P4, T4R, P2, T4L, P4, K3, P3, K2, C4F twice; repeat from ★ once **more**, P1.

Row 6: Slip 1 as if to **knit**, P 10, ★ K3, P3, (K4, P3) 3 times, K3, P 10; repeat from ★ once **more**, K1.

Row 7: Slip 1 as if to **purl**, C4B twice, K2, ★ P3, K3, (P4, K3) 3 times, P3, C4B twice, K2; repeat from ★ once **more**, P1.

Row 8: Repeat Row 6.

Row 9: Slip 1 as if to **purl**, K2, C4F twice, ★ P3, K3, P4, T4L, P2, T4R, P4, K3, P3, K2, C4F twice; repeat from ★ once **more**, P1.

Row 10: Repeat Row 4.

Instructions continued on page 42.

Row 11: Slip 1 as if to **purl**, C4B twice, K2, ★ P3, K3, P5, T4L, T4R, P5, K3, P3, C4B twice, K2; repeat from ★ once **more**, P1.

Row 12: Slip 1 as if to **knit**, P 10, ★ K3, P3, K6, P6, K6, P3, K3, P 10; repeat from ★ once **more**, K1.

Row 13: Slip 1 as if to **purl**, K2, C4F twice, ★ P3, K3, P6, C6B, P6, K3, P3, K2, C4F twice; repeat from ★ once **more**, P1.

Row 14: Repeat Row 12.

Row 15: Slip 1 as if to **purl**, C4B twice, K2, ★ P3, (T4L, P4, T4R) twice, P3, C4B twice, K2; repeat from ★ once **more**, P1.

Row 16: Slip 1 as if to **knit**, P 10, ★ (K4, P3) twice, K2, (P3, K4) twice, P 10; repeat from ★ once **more**, K1.

Row 17: Slip 1 as if to **purl**, K2, C4F twice, ★ P4, T4L, P2, T4R, P2, T4L, P2, T4R, P4, K2, C4F twice; repeat from ★ once **more**, P1.

Row 18: Slip 1 as if to **knit**, P 10, ★ K5, P3, K2, P3, K4, P3, K2, P3, K5, P 10; repeat from ★ once **more**, K1.

Row 19: Slip 1 as if to **purl**, C4B twice, K2, ★ P5, T4L, T4R, P4, T4L, T4R, P5, C4B twice, K2; repeat from ★ once **more**, P1.

Row 20: Slip 1 as if to **knit**, P 10, ★ K6, (P6, K6) twice, P 10; repeat from ★ once **more**, K1.

Row 21: Slip 1 as if to **purl**, K2, C4F twice, ★ P6, (C6F, P6) twice, K2, C4F twice; repeat from ★ once **more**, P1.

Row 22: Repeat Row 20.

Row 23: Slip 1 as if to **purl**, C4B twice, K2, ★ P5, T4R, T4L, P4, T4R, T4L, P5, C4B twice, K2; repeat from ★ once **more**, P1.

Row 24: Repeat Row 18.

Row 25: Slip 1 as if to **purl**, K2, C4F twice, ★ P4, T4R, P2, T4L, P2, T4R, P2, T4L, P4, K2, C4F twice; repeat from ★ once **more**, P1.

Row 26: Repeat Row 16.

Row 27: Slip 1 as if to **purl**, C4B twice, K2, ★ P3, (T4R, P4, T4L) twice, P3, C4B twice, K2; repeat from ★ once **more**, P1.

Rows 28-44: Repeat Rows 12-27 once, then repeat Row 12 once **more**.

Rows 45-56: Repeat Rows 1-12.

Rows 57-393: Repeat Rows 1-56, 6 times; then repeat Row 1 once **more**.

Bind off all sts in pattern.

FRINGE

Holding 6 strands of yarn together, each 28" (71 cm) long, add fringe to short edges of Shawl *(Figs. 11a & b, page 94)*, beginning 3 sts in from edge and repeating until there are 9 fringes evenly spaced across. Divide strands and knot evenly across twice *(Figs. 11c & d, page 94)*.

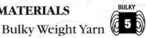 INTERMEDIATE

Finished Size: see page 46

MATERIALS

BULKY
5

Bulky Weight Yarn
[3.5 ounces, 198 yards
(100 grams, 180 meters)
per skein]: 2{3-3-4} skeins
Contrasting color smooth Bulky
Weight Yarn for crochet chain
cast on (waste yarn): 10 yards
(9 meters)
47" (119.5 cm) Circular knitting
needle, size 10 (6 mm) **or** size
needed for gauge
Double pointed needle, size 6
(4 mm)
Marker
Crochet hook, size K (6.5 mm)

Joan Beebe
The möbius strip
is a continuous
band with a single
twist connecting
inner and outer
surfaces. It's also a
symbol for eternity.
To let someone
know you always
wish her well, knit
Joan's möbius shrug
in her favorite hues.

*Photo model made
using Araucania Azapa
#808 Sea Green.*

*Instructions continued
on page 46.*

Size	Finished Measurement
Small:	38" circumference x 10^1/$_4$" long (96.5 cm x 26 cm)
Medium:	42^1/$_2$" circumference x 10^1/$_4$" long (108 cm x 26 cm)
Large:	47" circumference x 10^1/$_4$" long (119.5 cm x 26 cm)
X-Large:	51^1/$_4$" circumference x 10^1/$_4$" long (130 cm x 26 cm)

Size Note: Instructions are written for size Small with sizes Medium, Large, and X-Large in braces { }. Instructions will be easier to read if you circle all the numbers pertaining to your size. If only one number is given, it applies to all sizes.

GAUGE: In Stockinette Stitch, 14 sts and 19 rows = 4" (10 cm)

Techniques used: • YO *(Figs. 3a & b, pages 88 and 89)*; • Slip 1 as if to **knit**, K2, PSSO *(Fig. 8, page 92)*; • Slip 1 as if to **purl**, P2, PSSO *(Figs. 9a & b, page 92)*; and • K2 tog *(Fig. 4, page 90)*

With crochet hook and waste yarn, chain 138{154-170-186}; finish off *(see Crochet Stitches, page 95)*.

Using circular needle and beginning in **last** chain made, pick up one st in the back ridge of each chain across *(Fig. A)*: 138{154-170-186} sts.

Fig. A

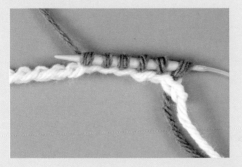

Instructions continued on page 48.

Place marker to mark beginning of round *(see Markers, page 87)*. Making sure beginning chain is not twisted *(Fig. B)* and working **behind** sts on left point, insert double pointed needle from **back** to **front** in bottom loop between first 2 sts, ★ [insert double pointed needle from **back** to **front** in bottom loop between next 2 sts] 4 to 6 times *(Fig. C)*, then knit sts from double pointed needle *(Fig. D)*; repeat from ★ around: 275{307-339-371} sts.

Fig. B

Fig. C

Fig. E

Cable

The cable portion of your needle is doubled and should **not** be twisted *(Fig. E)*. Release the finished off end of chain and pull to unzip chain *(Fig. F)*. As you begin to knit, the cable will cross **once**. Notice that there is a garter ridge on the back of your work.

Fig. F

Instructions continued on page 50.

Foundation Rnd: Knit into the front **and** into the back of the first st, knit around to marker. There is a garter ridge on each side of the work: 276{308-340-372} sts.

Rnd 1: (K2, P2) around.

Rnd 2: ★ K1, YO, K1, P1, YO, P1; repeat from ★ around: 414{462-510-558} sts.

Rnd 3: (K3, P3) around.

Rnd 4: ★ Slip 1 as if to **knit**, K2, PSSO, slip 1 as if to **purl**, P2, PSSO; repeat from ★ around: 276{308-340-372} sts.

Rnd 5: (K2, P2) around.

Rnd 6: Knit around.

Rnd 7: Purl around.

Rnds 8-10: Repeat Rnds 1-3: 414{462-510-558} sts.

Rnd 11: ★ K2, slip 2 sts just worked to left needle, insert right needle into third st on left needle and pass it over first 2 sts and off the needle, slip 2 sts back to right needle, P2, slip 2 sts just worked to left needle, insert right needle into third st on left needle and pass it over first 2 sts and off the needle, slip 2 sts back to right needle; repeat from ★ around: 276{308-340-372} sts.

Rnds 12-14: Repeat Rnds 5-7.

Rnds 15-28: Repeat Rnds 1-14.

Rnd 29: (YO, K2 tog) around.

Rnd 30: Purl around.

Bind off all sts in **knit**.

 **INTERMEDIATE**

Finished Size: 18"w x 62¹/₂"l
(45.5 cm x 159 cm)

MATERIALS

Bulky Weight Yarn
[3.5 ounces, 120 yards
(100 grams, 110 meters)
per skein]: 7 skeins
Straight knitting needles, size
10 (6 mm) **or** size needed
for gauge
Cable needle

Judy Lamb
This sweet shawl is
rich with texture!
Judy's cable pattern
seems to untwist in
segments, allowing
openwork spaces
to show through.
Bulky yarn and
caring thoughts
make this shawl
extra-warm.

*Photo model made
using Bernat® Alpaca
Natural Blends #93011
Wheat.*

*Instructions continued
on page 54.*

GAUGE: In pattern, 17 sts and 21 rows = 4" (10 cm)

Techniques used: • YO *(Fig. 3a, page 88)*; • K2 tog *(Fig. 4, page 90)*; and • SSK *(Figs. 10a-c, page 93)*

STITCH GUIDE

CABLE (uses 5 sts)
Slip next 3 sts onto cable needle and hold in **back** of work, K2 from left needle, K3 from cable needle.

BODY

Cast on 78 sts.

Rows 1-4: Knit across.

Row 5: K3, P2, ★ K1, (YO, K2 tog) twice, P2, K5, P2; repeat from ★ across, K3.

Row 6 AND ALL WRONG SIDE ROWS: K5, P5, (K2, P5) across to last 5 sts, K5.

Row 7: K3, P2, ★ K1, (YO, K2 tog) twice, P2, K5, P2; repeat from ★ across, K3.

Row 9: K3, P2, ★ K1, (YO, K2 tog) twice, P2, work Cable, P2; repeat from ★ across to last 3 sts, K3.

Rows 11-18: Repeat Rows 5-10 once, then repeat Rows 5 and 6 once **more**.

Row 19: K3, P2, ★ K5, P2, (SSK, YO) twice, K1, P2; repeat from ★ across to last 3 sts, K3.

Row 21: K3, P2, ★ K5, P2, (SSK, YO) twice, K1, P2; repeat from ★ across to last 3 sts, K3

Row 23: K3, P2, ★ work Cable, P2, (SSK, YO) twice, K1, P2; repeat from ★ across to last 3 sts, K3.

Rows 25-32: Repeat Rows 19-24 once, then repeat Rows 19 and 20 once **more**.

Rows 33-325: Repeat Rows 5-32, 10 times; then repeat Rows 5-17 once **more**.

Rows 326-329: Knit across.

Bind off all sts in **knit**.

Tranquil Waves

◖■■■▭ INTERMEDIATE

Finished Size: 21¹/₂"w x 68"l
(54.5 cm x 172.5 cm)

MATERIALS

Medium Weight Yarn
[3 ounces, 197 yards
(85 grams, 180 meters)
per skein]:
Lt Grey - 3 skeins
Dk Grey - 3 skeins
29" (73.5 cm) Circular knitting
needle, size 10 (6 mm) **or** size
needed for gauge
Crochet hook, size I (5.5 mm)
for edging

Judy Lamb
Like ripples on the
water, your prayers
on her behalf will
spread through the
fabric of the shawl
you create. Choose
two shades of her
favorite color to
make your own
version of Judy's
toasty wrap.

*Photo model made
using Lion Brand®
Wool-Ease® #151 Grey
Heather and #152
Oxford Grey.*

*Instructions continued
on page 58.*

GAUGE: In pattern, 20 sts and 32 rows = 4" (10 cm)

Note: When instructed to slip stitches, always slip as if to **purl** with yarn held **loosely** on **wrong** side of work. Carry yarn not being used **loosely** along side edge, picking up new color from beneath the dropped color.

BODY

With Lt Grey, cast on 341 sts.

Row 1: Purl across, drop Lt Grey.

Row 2 (Right side)**:** With Dk Grey, K9, slip 2, K7, slip 2, ★ K 15, slip 2, K7, slip 2; repeat from ★ across to last 9 sts, K9.

Row 3: K9, slip 2, P7, slip 2, ★ K 15, slip 2, P7, slip 2; repeat from ★ across to last 9 sts, K9, drop Dk Grey.

Row 4: With Lt Grey, K2, (slip 1, K1) twice, slip 1, K4, slip 2, K3, slip 2, K4, ★ (slip 1, K1) 5 times, slip 1, K4, slip 2, K3, slip 2, K4; repeat from ★ across to last 7 sts, (slip 1, K1) twice, slip 1, K2.

Row 5: K2, (slip 1, K1) twice, slip 1, P4, slip 2, K3, slip 2, P4, ★ (slip 1, K1) 5 times, slip 1, P4, slip 2, K3, slip 2, P4; repeat from ★ across to last 7 sts, (slip 1, K1) twice, slip 1, K2, drop Lt Grey.

Row 6: With Dk Grey, K7, slip 2, K4, slip 1, K1, slip 1, K4, slip 2, ★ K 11, slip 2, K4, slip 1, K1, slip 1, K4, slip 2; repeat from ★ across to last 7 sts, K7.

Row 7: K7, slip 2, P4, slip 1, K1, slip 1, P4, slip 2, ★ K 11, slip 2, P4, slip 1, K1, slip 1, P4, slip 2; repeat from ★ across to last 7 sts, K7, drop Dk Grey.

Row 8: With Lt Grey, K2, slip 1, K1, slip 1, K4, slip 2, K7, slip 2, K4, ★ (slip 1, K1) 3 times, slip 1, K4, slip 2, K7, slip 2, K4; repeat from ★ across to last 5 sts, slip 1, K1, slip 1, K2.

Row 9: K2, slip 1, K1, slip 1, P4, slip 2, K7, slip 2, P4, ★ (slip 1, K1) 3 times, slip 1, P4, slip 2, K7, slip 2, P4; repeat from ★ across to last 5 sts, slip 1, K1, slip 1, K2, drop Lt Grey.

Row 10: With Dk Grey, K5, slip 2, K4, (slip 1, K1) 3 times, slip 1, K4, slip 2, ★ K7, slip 2, K4, (slip 1, K1) 3 times, slip 1, K4, slip 2; repeat from ★ across to last 5 sts, K5.

Row 11: K5, slip 2, P4, (slip 1, K1) 3 times, slip 1, P4, slip 2, ★ K7, slip 2, P4, (slip 1, K1) 3 times, slip 1, P4, slip 2; repeat from ★ across to last 5 sts, K5, drop Dk Grey.

Instructions continued on page 60.

Row 12: With Lt Grey, K2, slip 1, K4, slip 2, K 11, slip 2, K4, slip 1, ★ K1, slip 1, K4, slip 2, K 11, slip 2, K4, slip 1; repeat from ★ across to last 2 sts, K2.

Row 13: K2, slip 1, P4, slip 2, K 11, slip 2, P4, slip 1, ★ K1, slip 1, P4, slip 2, K 11, slip 2, P4, slip 1; repeat from ★ across to last 2 sts, K2, drop Lt Grey.

Row 14: With Dk Grey, K3, ★ slip 2, K4, (slip 1, K1) 5 times, slip 1, K4, slip 2, K3; repeat from ★ across.

Row 15: K3, ★ slip 2, P4, (slip 1, K1) 5 times, slip 1, P4, slip 2, K3; repeat from ★ across, drop Dk Grey.

Row 16: With Lt Grey, K5, slip 2, K 15, slip 2, ★ K7, slip 2, K 15, slip 2; repeat from ★ across to last 5 sts, K5.

Row 17: P5, slip 2, K 15, slip 2, ★ P7, slip 2, K 15, slip 2; repeat from ★ across to last 5 sts, P5, drop Lt Grey.

Row 18: With Dk Grey, K2, slip 1, K8, slip 2, K3, slip 2, K8, slip 1, ★ K1, slip 1, K8, slip 2, K3, slip 2, K8, slip 1; repeat from ★ across to last 2 sts, K2.

Row 19: K2, slip 1, P8, slip 2, P3, slip 2, P8, slip 1, ★ K1, slip 1, P8, slip 2, P3, slip 2, P8, slip 1; repeat from ★ across to last 2 sts, K2, drop Dk Grey.

Row 20: With Lt Grey, K3, ★ slip 2, K8, slip 1, K1, slip 1, K8, slip 2, K3; repeat from ★ across.

Row 21: P3, ★ slip 2, P8, slip 1, K1, slip 1, P8, slip 2, P3; repeat from ★ across, drop Lt Grey.

Rows 22-161: Repeat Rows 2-21, 7 times.

Cut Dk Grey yarn. Bind off all sts in **knit** with Lt Grey, place last loop onto crochet hook *(see Crochet Stitches, pages 95 and 96)*.

EDGING

Rnd 1: With Dk Grey and crochet hook, ch 1, ★ work 3 sc in corner of Body, sc in end of every Dk Grey row across short end, work 3 sc in next corner st, sc in every other st across long edge; repeat from ★ once **more**; join with slip st to first sc.

Rnd 2: Ch 1, do **not** turn; working Back Loops Only, sc in same st and in each sc around; join with slip st to **both** loops of first sc, finish off.

Nature's peace

■■■▭ INTERMEDIATE

Finished Size: 20"w x 46"l
(51 cm x 117 cm)

MATERIALS

Medium Weight Yarn
[3 ounces, 185 yards
(85 grams, 170 meters)
per skein]:
    Brown - 4 skeins
    Lt Green - 2 skeins
    Dk Green - 1 skein
24" (61 cm) Circular knitting
    needle, size 9 (5.5 mm) **or**
    size needed for gauge

Karen Ratto-Whooley
A favorite pattern to knit, ripples are also fun to wear. Karen's soothing shawl takes its colors from nature. It also contains the extra comfort of prayers and good wishes.

Photo model made using Caron® Country #0015 Deep Taupe, #0012 Foliage, and #0020 Loden Forest.

Instructions continued on page 64.

GAUGE: In Stockinette Stitch,
16 sts and 22 rows = 4" (10 cm)

Techniques used: • Slip 1 as if to **knit**, K2 tog, PSSO *(Figs. 6a & b, page 91)*; • YO *(Figs. 3a & b, pages 88 and 89)*; and • P2 tog *(Fig. 5, page 90)*

FIRST END

With Lt Green, cast on 111 sts.

Row 1 (Right side): K2, purl across to last 2 sts, K2.

Row 2: Knit across.

Row 3: K2, purl across to last 2 sts, K2.

Row 4: K2, (P2 tog, YO) across to last 3 sts, P1, K2.

Rows 5 and 6: Knit across.

Row 7: K2, purl across to last 2 sts, K2.

Row 8: Knit across, cut Lt Green.

Row 9: With Brown, K2, ★ † YO, K4, slip 1 as if to **knit**, K2 tog, PSSO, K4, YO †, K1; repeat from ★ across to last 13 sts, then repeat from † to † once, K2.

Row 10: K2, purl across to last 2 sts, K2.

Rows 11-19: Repeat Rows 9 and 10, 4 times; then repeat Row 9 once **more**; at end of Row 19, cut Brown.

Row 20: With Dk Green, K2, purl across to last 2 sts, K2.

Row 21: K2, purl across to last 2 sts, K2.

Row 22: Knit across.

Row 23: K2, purl across to last 2 sts, K2.

Row 24: K2, (P2 tog, YO) across to last 3 sts, P1, K2.

Rows 25 and 26: Knit across.

Row 27: K2, purl across to last 2 sts, K2.

Row 28: Knit across, cut Dk Green.

Rows 29-39: Repeat Rows 9 and 10, 5 times; then repeat Row 9 once **more**; at end of Row 39, cut Brown.

Instructions continued on page 83.

Sweet solace

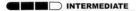

 INTERMEDIATE

Kay Meadors

A sweep of coral that ends in a point on the back and is long enough to tie in the front, Kay's comforting design alternates solid stripes with an openweave pattern.

Finished Size: 58"w x 30"l (147.5 cm x 76 cm) unblocked 70"w x 37"l (178 cm x 94 cm) blocked

MATERIALS

Medium Weight Yarn **MEDIUM 4**
[3 ounces, 185 yards (85 grams, 170 meters) per skein]: 3 skeins
24" (61 cm) Circular knitting needle, size 10 (6 mm) **or** size needed for gauge
Marker

Photo model made using Caron® Country #0002 Coral Lipstick.

Instructions continued on page 68.

GAUGE: In Stockinette Stitch,
 16 sts and 20 rows = 4" (10 cm)

Techniques used: • Increase *(Figs. 1a & b, page 87)*;
• YO *(Fig. 3a, page 88)*; • K2 tog *(Fig. 4, page 90)*; and
• SSK *(Figs. 10a-c, page 93)*

BODY

Cast on 7 sts.

Rows 1-3: Knit across.

Row 4 (Right side)**:** K2, YO, increase, place marker *(see Markers, page 87)*, increase, K1, YO, K2: 11 sts.

Row 5: K2, purl across to last 2 sts, K2.

Row 6: K2, YO, K2, increase, slip marker, increase, K3, YO, K2: 15 sts.

Row 7: K2, purl across to last 2 sts, K2.

Row 8: K2, YO, knit across to within one st of marker, increase, slip marker, increase, knit across to last 2 sts, YO, K2: 19 sts.

Row 9: K2, purl across to last 2 sts, K2.

Rows 10-23: Repeat Rows 8 and 9, 7 times: 47 sts.

Row 24: K2, YO, (K2 tog, YO) across to within one st of marker, K1, YO, slip marker, K1 **(center st)**, YO, K1, (YO, SSK) across to last 2 sts, YO, K2: 51 sts.

Row 25: K2, purl across to last 2 sts, K2.

Rows 26-43: Repeat Rows 24 and 25, 9 times: 87 sts.

Rows 44-63: Repeat Rows 8 and 9, 10 times: 127 sts.

Rows 64-83: Repeat Rows 24 and 25, 10 times: 167 sts.

Rows 84-103: Repeat Rows 8 and 9, 10 times: 207 sts.

Rows 104-138: Repeat Rows 24 and 25, 17 times; then repeat Row 24 once **more**: 279 sts.

Bind off all sts **loosely** in **knit**.

Block Shawl to finished size.

◼◼◻◻ EASY +

Finished Size: 52¹/₂"w x 55³/₄"l
(133.5 cm x 141.5 cm)

MATERIALS
Bulky Weight Yarn
[6 ounces, 185 yards
(170 grams, 169 meters)
per skein]: 4 skeins
Straight knitting needles, size 11
(8 mm) **or** size needed
for gauge

Kay Meadors
If you've ever
wished you could
completely wrap
a loved one in
your prayers, knit
Kay's ruana for that
special someone.
The generous
width of this shawl
makes it as warm
and inviting as a
lap blanket.

*Photo model made
using Lion Brand®
Homespun® #301
Shaker.*

*Instructions continued
on page 72.*

GAUGE: In Stockinette Stitch, 10 sts and 14 rows = 4" (10 cm)

Techniques used: • Increase *(Figs. 1a & b, page 87)*;
• SSK *(Figs. 10a-c, page 93)*; and • K2 tog *(Fig. 4, page 90)*

BACK

Cast on 71 sts.

Rows 1-4: K1, (P1, K1) across.

Row 5: K1, P1, K1, purl across to last 3 sts, K1, P1, K1.

Row 6 (Right side): K1, P1, increase, knit across to last 4 sts, increase, K1, P1, K1: 73 sts.

Row 7: K1, P1, K1, purl across to last 3 sts, K1, P1, K1.

Rows 8-65: Repeat Rows 6 and 7, 29 times: 131 sts.

Row 66: K1, P1, knit across to last 2 sts, P1, K1.

Row 67: K1, P1, K1, purl across to last 3 sts, K1, P1, K1.

Rows 68-95: Repeat Rows 66 and 67, 14 times.

Row 96: K1, P1, K 56, P1, (K1, P1) 7 times, knit across to last 2 sts, P1, K1.

Row 97: K1, P1, K1, P 54, K1, (P1, K1) 8 times, purl across to last 3 sts, K1, P1, K1.

Rows 98 and 99: Repeat Rows 96 and 97.

FRONT

Row 1 (Dividing row): K1, P1, K 56, P1, K1, bind off next 11 sts **loosely** in pattern; P1, knit across to last 2 sts, P1, K1: 60 sts **each** side.

Note: Both sides of Front are worked at the same time, using a separate skein of yarn for **each** side.

Row 2: K1, P1, K1, purl across to last 3 sts, K1, P1, K1; with second yarn, K1, P1, K1, purl across to last 3 sts, K1, P1, K1.

Row 3: K1, P1, knit across to last 2 sts, P1, K1; with second yarn, K1, P1, knit across to last 2 sts, P1, K1.

Rows 4-34: Repeat Rows 2 and 3, 15 times; then repeat Row 2 once **more**.

Instructions continued on page 84.

■■■◻ **INTERMEDIATE**

Finished Size: 11¹/₂"w x 60"l
(29 cm x 152.5 cm)

MATERIALS
Medium Weight Yarn
[3.5 ounces, 185 yards
(100 grams, 170 meters)
per hank]: 4 hanks
Straight knitting needles, size 9
(5.5 mm) **or** size needed
for gauge

Linda Lum DeBono

Linda used a fresh, green Leaf Stitch for this little shawl to create a sense of serenity. This peaceful gift will be welcomed for the friendship and caring you put into every stitch.

Photo model made using LB Collection® Organic Wool #134 Avocado.

Instructions continued on page 76.

GAUGE: In pattern, 19 sts and 28 rows = 4" (10 cm)

Techniques used: • Slip 1 as if to **knit**, K2 tog, PSSO *(Figs. 6a & b, page 91)*; • YO *(Fig. 3a, page 88)*; and • SSK *(Figs. 10a-c, page 93)*

BODY

Cast on 55 sts.

Rows 1 and 2: Knit across.

Row 3 AND ALL WRONG SIDE ROWS: K3, purl across to last 3 sts, K3.

Row 4: K4, ★ † YO, K2, slip 1 as if to **knit**, K2 tog, PSSO, K2, YO †, K1; repeat from ★ 4 times **more**, then repeat from † to † once, K4.

Row 6: K5, ★ †YO, K1, slip 1 as if to **knit**, K2 tog, PSSO, K1, YO †, K3; repeat from ★ 4 times **more**, then repeat from † to † once, K5.

Row 8: K6, ★ †YO, slip 1 as if to **knit**, K2 tog, PSSO, YO †, K5; repeat from ★ 4 times **more**, then repeat from † to † once, K6.

Row 10: K3, K2 tog, ★ † K2, YO, K1, YO, K2 †, slip 1 as if to **knit**, K2 tog, PSSO; repeat from ★ 4 times **more**, then repeat from † to † once, SSK, K3.

Row 12: K3, K2 tog, ★ † K1, YO, K3, YO, K1 †, slip 1 as if to **knit**, K2 tog, PSSO; repeat from ★ 4 times **more**, then repeat from † to † once, SSK, K3.

Row 14: K3, K2 tog, ★ †YO, K5, YO †, slip 1 as if to **knit**, K2 tog, PSSO; repeat from ★ 4 times **more**, then repeat from † to † once, SSK, K3.

Repeat Rows 3-14 for pattern until Body measures approximately 59³/₄" (152 cm) from cast on edge, ending by working Row 8 or Row 14.

Last 2 Rows: Knit across.

Bind off all sts in **knit**.

 **EASY +**

Finished Size: 73½"w x 45"d
(186.5 cm x 114.5 cm)
excluding fringe

MATERIALS

Medium Weight Yarn
[6 ounces, 335 yards
(170 grams, 306 meters)
per skein]: 3 skeins
36" (91.5 cm) Circular knitting
needle, size 7 (4.5 mm) **or**
size needed for gauge
Crochet hook for fringe

*Rita Weiss,
Creative
Partners, LLC.*
The full sweep
of this classically
stylish shawl is
further enhanced
by its long fringe.
The rosy hue
conveys prayers
for happiness and
good health.

*Photo model made
using TLC® Amoré™
#3710 Rose.*

*Instructions continued
on page 80.*

GAUGE: In pattern, 10 sts and16 rows = 4" (10 cm)

Techniques used: • Increase *(Figs. 1a & b, page 87)* and • YO twice *(Fig. A)*

Fig. A

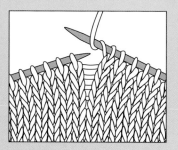

BODY

Cast on 4 sts.

Rows 1 and 2: Knit across.

Rows 3-5 (Increase rows): Increase, knit across to last st, increase: 10 sts.

Row 6: K1, (YO twice, K1) across: 28 sts.

Row 7: K1, (drop 2 YOs from needle, K1) across: 10 sts.

Gently tug on dropped sts so they lie flat.

Row 8: Knit across.

Rows 9-182: Repeat Rows 3-8, 29 times: 184 sts.

Bind off all sts **loosely** in **knit**.

FRINGE

Holding 4 strands of yarn together, each 12" (30.5 cm) long, add fringe to edges of Shawl *(Figs. 11a & b, page 94)*.

Instructions continued from Colors of Joy, page 37.

Row 31: K2, YO, K1, ★ †YO, K2, slip 1, K2 tog, PSSO, K2, YO †, K3; repeat from ★ across to last 10 sts, then repeat from † to † once, K1, YO, K2: 35 sts.

Row 33: K2, YO, K3, ★ †YO, K1, slip 1, K2 tog, PSSO, K1, YO †, K5; repeat from ★ across to last 10 sts, then repeat from † to † once, K3, YO, K2: 37 sts.

Row 35: K2, YO, K5, ★ †YO, slip 1, K2 tog, PSSO, YO †, K7; repeat from ★ across to last 10 sts, then repeat from † to † once, K5, YO, K2: 39 sts.

Row 37: K2, YO, K7, ★ YO, K1, YO, K3, slip 1, K2 tog, PSSO, K3; repeat from ★ across to last 10 sts, YO, K1, YO, K7, YO, K2: 43 sts.

Repeat Rows 30-37 until there are 11 complete leaf patterns down center of Shawl, ending by working Row 35.

Last 4 Rows: Knit across.

Bind off all sts in **knit**.

FRINGE

Holding 3 strands of yarn together, each 10" (25.5 cm) long, add fringe in every other YO along both sides of Shawl *(Figs. 11a & b, page 94)*.

Row 40: With Lt Green, K2, purl across to last 2 sts, K2.

Rows 41-88: Repeat Rows 1-40 once, then repeat Rows 1-8 once **more**.

BODY

Repeat Rows 9 and 10 for pattern until piece measures 36" (91.5 cm) from cast on edge, ending by working Row 10.

SECOND END

Rows 1-88: Repeat Rows 1-88 of First End.

Bind off all sts in pattern of Row 9 so that ripple will remain intact.

Instructions continued from Restful Ruana, page 73.

Row 35 (Decrease row): K1, P1, SSK, knit across to last 2 sts, P1, K1; with second yarn, K1, P1, knit across to last 4 sts, K2 tog, P1, K1: 59 sts **each** side.

Row 36: K1, P1, K1, purl across to last 3 sts, K1, P1, K1; with second yarn, K1, P1, K1, purl across to last 3 sts, K1, P1, K1.

Rows 37-92: Repeat Rows 35 and 36, 28 times: 31 sts **each** side.

Rows 93-96: K1, (P1, K1) across; with second yarn, K1, (P1, K1) across.

Bind off all sts **loosely** in pattern.

general instructions

ABBREVIATIONS

C4B	Cable 4 Back
C4F	Cable 4 Front
C6B	Cable 6 Back
C6F	Cable 6 Front
ch(s)	chain(s)
cm	centimeters
K	knit
M1	make one
mm	millimeters
P	purl
PSSO	pass slipped stitch over
Rnd(s)	Round(s)
sc	single crochet(s)
SSK	slip, slip, knit
st(s)	stitch(es)
T4L	Twist 4 Left
T4R	Twist 4 Right
tog	together
YO	yarn over

★ — work instructions following ★ as **many more** times as indicated in addition to the first time.

† to † — work all instructions from first † to second † **as many** times as specified.

( ) or [ ] — work enclosed instructions **as many** times as specified by the number immediately following **or** contains explanatory remarks.

colon (:) — the number(s) given after a colon at the end of a row or round denote(s) the number of stitches you should have on that row or round.

KNITTING NEEDLES

UNITED STATES	ENGLISH U.K.	METRIC (mm)
0	13	2
1	12	2.25
2	11	2.75
3	10	3.25
4	9	3.5
5	8	3.75
6	7	4
7	6	4.5
8	5	5
9	4	5.5
10	3	6
10½	2	6.5
11	1	8
13	00	9
15	000	10
17	---	12.75

KNIT TERMINOLOGY

UNITED STATES		INTERNATIONAL
gauge	=	tension
bind off	=	cast off
yarn over (YO)	=	yarn forward (yfwd) **or** yarn around needle (yrn)

Yarn Weight Symbol & Names	SUPER FINE 1	FINE 2	LIGHT 3	MEDIUM 4	BULKY 5	SUPER BULKY 6
Type of Yarns in Category	Sock, Fingering Baby	Sport, Baby	DK, Light Worsted	Worsted, Afghan, Aran	Chunky, Craft, Rug	Bulky, Roving
Knit Gauge Ranges in Stockinette St to 4" (10 cm)	27-32 sts	23-26 sts	21-24 sts	16-20 sts	12-15 sts	6-11 sts
Advised Needle Size Range	1-3	3-5	5-7	7-9	9-11	11 and larger

■□□□ BEGINNER	Projects for first-time knitters using basic knit and purl stitches. Minimal shaping.
■■□□ EASY	Projects using basic stitches, repetitive stitch patterns, simple color changes, and simple shaping and finishing.
■■■□ INTERMEDIATE	Projects with a variety of stitches, such as basic cables and lace, simple intarsia, double-pointed needles and knitting in the round needle techniques, mid-level shaping and finishing.
■■■■ EXPERIENCED	Projects using advanced techniques and stitches, such as short rows, fair isle, more intricate intarsia, cables, lace patterns, and numerous color changes.

GAUGE

Exact gauge is **essential** for proper size. Before beginning your Shawl, make a sample swatch in the yarn and needle specified. After completing the swatch, measure it, counting your stitches and rows carefully. If your swatch is larger or smaller than specified, **make another, changing needle size to get the correct gauge**. Keep trying until you find the size needles that will give you the specified gauge. Once proper gauge is obtained, measure width of Shawl approximately every 3" (7.5 cm) to be sure gauge remains consistent.

If you have more rows per inch than specified, use a larger size needle for the purl rows; if fewer, use a smaller size needle for the purl rows.

MARKERS

As a convenience to you, we have used markers to help distinguish the beginning of a pattern or a round. Place markers as instructed. You may use purchased markers or tie a length of contrasting color yarn around the needle. When you reach a marker on each row, slip it from the left needle to the right needle; remove it when no longer needed.

INCREASE

Knit the next stitch but do **not** slip the old stitch off the left needle *(Fig. 1a)*. Insert the right needle into the **back** loop of the **same** stitch and knit it *(Fig. 1b)*, then slip the old stitch off the left needle.

Fig. 1a   **Fig. 1b**

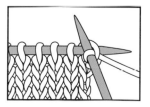
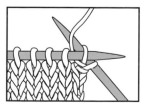

MAKE ONE *(abbreviated M1)*

Insert the **left** needle under the horizontal strand between the stitches from the front *(Fig. 2a)*. Then knit into the **back** of the strand *(Fig. 2b)*.

Fig. 2a

Fig. 2b

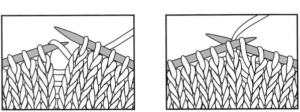

YARN OVER *(abbreviated YO)*

After a knit stitch, before a knit stitch

Bring the yarn forward **between** the needles, then back **over** the top of the right hand needle, so that it is now in position to knit the next stitch *(Fig. 3a)*.

Fig. 3a

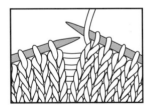

After a purl stitch, before a purl stitch

Take the yarn over the right hand needle to the back, then forward under it, so that it is now in position to purl the next stitch *(Fig. 3b)*.

Fig. 3b

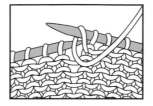

After a knit stitch, before a purl stitch

Bring the yarn forward between the needles, then back over the top of the right hand needle and forward between the needles again, so that it is now in position to purl the next stitch *(Fig. 3c)*.

Fig. 3c

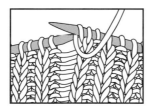

After a purl stitch, before a knit stitch

Take the yarn **over** right hand needle to the back, so that it is now in position to knit the next stitch *(Fig. 3d)*.

Fig. 3d

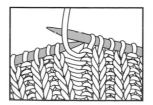

KNIT 2 TOGETHER *(abbreviated K2 tog)*

Insert the right needle into the **front** of the first two stitches on the left needle as if to **knit** *(Fig. 4)*, then **knit** them together as if they were one stitch.

Fig. 4

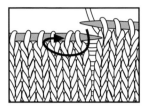

PURL 2 TOGETHER *(abbreviated P2 tog)*

Insert the right needle into the **front** of the first two stitches on the left needle as if to **purl** *(Fig. 5)*, then **purl** them together as if they were one stitch.

Fig. 5

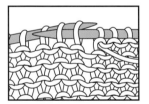

SLIP 1, KNIT 2 TOGETHER, PASS SLIPPED STITCH OVER
(abbreviated slip 1, K2 tog, PSSO)

Slip one stitch as if to **knit** *(Fig. 6a)*, K2 tog *(Fig. 4)*. With the left needle, bring the slipped stitch over the stitch just made *(Fig. 6b)* and off the needle.

Fig. 6a   **Fig. 6b**

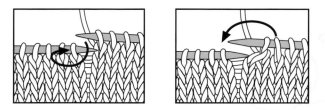

SLIP 1, KNIT 1, PASS SLIPPED STITCH OVER *(abbreviated slip 1, K1, PSSO)*

Slip one stitch as if to **knit**. Knit the next stitch. With the left needle, bring the slipped stitch over the knit stitch *(Fig. 7)* and off the needle.

Fig. 7

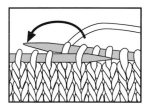

SLIP 1, KNIT 2, PASS SLIPPED
STITCH OVER *(abbreviated slip 1, K2, PSSO)*

Slip one stitch as if to **knit**. Knit the next two stitches. With the left needle, bring the slipped stitch over the two knit stitches *(Fig. 8)* and off the needle.

Fig. 8

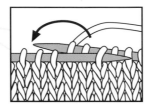

SLIP 1, PURL 2, PASS SLIPPED
STITCH OVER *(abbreviated slip 1, P2, PSSO)*

Slip one stitch as if to **purl** *(Fig. 9a)*. Purl the next two stitches. With the left needle, bring the slipped stitch over the two purl stitches *(Fig. 9b)* and off the needle.

Fig. 9a

Fig. 9b

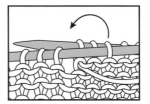

SLIP, SLIP, KNIT *(abbreviated SSK)*

Separately slip two stitches as if to **knit** *(Fig. 10a)*. Insert the left needle into the **front** of both slipped stitches *(Fig. 10b)* and knit them together as if they were one stitch *(Fig. 10c)*.

Fig. 10a

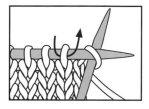

Fig. 10b

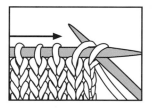

Fig. 10c

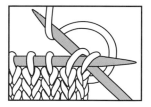

FRINGE

Cut a piece of cardboard 8" (20.5 cm) wide and half as long as length specified in individual instructions. Wind the yarn **loosely** and evenly around the cardboard lengthwise until the card is filled, then cut across one end; repeat as needed.

Step 1: Hold together as many strands of yarn as specified for the finished fringe; fold in half. With **wrong** side facing and using a crochet hook, draw the folded end up through a stitch or space and pull the loose ends through the folded end *(Fig. 11a)*; draw the knot up **tightly** *(Fig. 11b)*. Repeat spacing as specified.

Step 2: Divide each group in half and knot together with half of next group *(Fig. 11c)*.

Step 3: Separate each group in same manner and knot again *(Fig. 11d)*.

After completing step(s) specified in individual instructions, lay Shawl flat on a hard surface and trim the ends.

Fig. 11a

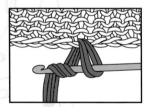

Fig. 11b

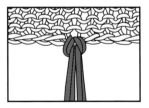

Fig. 11c

Fig. 11d

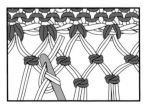

CROCHET STITCHES
CHAIN

To work a chain stitch, begin with a slip knot on the hook.
Bring the yarn **over** hook from back to front, catching the
yarn with the hook and turning the hook slightly toward you
to keep the yarn from slipping off. Draw the yarn through the
slip knot *(Fig. 12)* (**first chain st made,** *abbreviated ch*).

Fig. 12

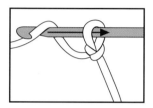

SLIP STITCH

To work a slip stitch, insert hook in stitch indicated, YO
and draw through st and through loop on hook *(Fig. 13)*
(**slip stitch made,** *abbreviated slip st*).

Fig. 13

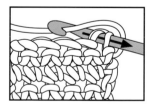

SINGLE CROCHET

Insert hook in stitch indicated, YO and pull up a loop, YO and draw through both loops on hook *(Fig. 14)* (**single crochet made,** *abbreviated sc*).

Fig. 14

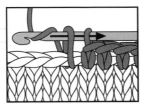

BACK LOOP ONLY

Work only in loop(s) indicated by arrow *(Fig. 15)*.

Fig. 15

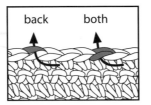